Buried in the Mind's Backyard

W.M. Rivera

Copyright © W.M. Rivera, 2011 All rights reserved.
No part of this book may be reproduced in any manner without written permission except in the case of brief quotations embodied in critical articles or reviews.

Editor: Clarinda Harriss
Graphic design: Ace Kieffer
Author photo: S.C. Stanley

Cover originally published by Blue Man Press, Paris. Image by Miguel Condé, Mexican figurative painter, draftsman and etcher: http://www.miguelconde.info

BrickHouse Books, Inc. 2011
306 Suffolk Road
Baltimore, MD 21218

Distributor: Itasca Books, Inc.
© 2011

ISBN: 978-1-935916-04-8

Acknowledgments

The author is grateful to the editors of the following magazine where these poems originally appeared:

"Delmore Schwartz" in *California Quarterly* 2010, 35:4, p. 28.

Honorable Mention for "Eros and Thanatos" in the 24th annual CSPS (California State Poetry Society) Poetry Contest.

"Mortality" in *Gargoyle* 2010, #56, p. 143.

"My Grandmother at the library" in *Kenyon Review* 1965, XXVII:1, Winter, p. 71.

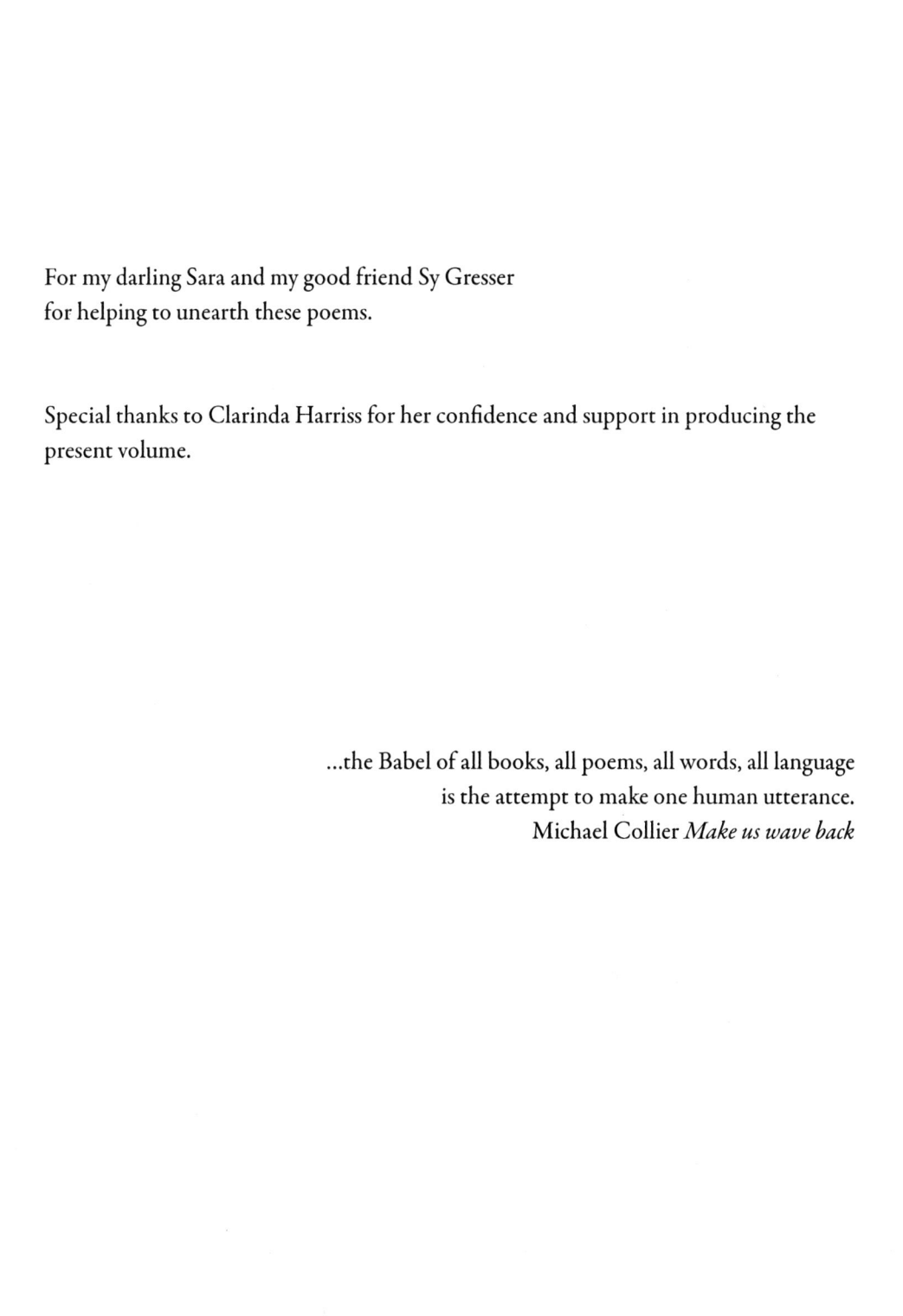

For my darling Sara and my good friend Sy Gresser
for helping to unearth these poems.

Special thanks to Clarinda Harriss for her confidence and support in producing the present volume.

> ...the Babel of all books, all poems, all words, all language
> is the attempt to make one human utterance.
> Michael Collier *Make us wave back*

Contents

I. BURIED IN THE MIND'S BACKYARD

Hurricane 15

Alfalfa... 16

Off to no ends 17

Noninferential 18

Gossip and black robes... 19

Triolet.. 20

Two kids beneath their parents' robes 21

Ice boiling 22

Heirs to Catullus.. 23

Hawking news to hurried cars 24

Thanksgiving.. 25

Lifeguard on duty 26

Buried in the mind's backyard 27

Disillusionment of the movie usher 28

My Grandmother at the Library 29

Spyglass hotel 30

Bones and Lavish... 31

Home-leave... 33

Icy stairs.. 34

Unfinished sestina 35

New Orleans and the Neighborhood....................... 37

Motherboard 38

New Orleans April 39

Deeper than the grave... 40

Where did it go? 43

Our lady of prompt succor 44

Winter firewood 45

Mortality 46

Fighting in the streets, Paris '68 47

The honey hardened 49

Weekends 50

Middle of nowhere 51

One wave goodbye 52

On the train and off what's left is time 53

Persimmons 54

Icarus again 55

II. RED WINTER

Red winter 58

Daisies 59

Everything I told her 60

Outstanding in Penn Station 61

In line at the grocery 62

She walks into the room 63

"The Carnal Prayer Mat" 64

Marie-Denise Villiers: self-portrait 66

Delmore Schwartz 67

"Lottery dream" 68

Angel bird 69

What's more difficult? 71

Broken mirror 73

Graffiti 74

Western Wind, the corollary 75

Patuxent River flow 76

Storm's edge 77

In the house alone 78

Eros and Thanatos 79

Spring's already here! 80

Beyond belief 81

Conch shell 82

In others' words 83

Notes 84

Bio 86

I. BURIED IN THE MIND'S BACKYARD

Hurricane

As if the spirit split open. Standing
In the doorway the hurricane rattles
the shutters flap and bang--the body spellbound,
life not yet autobiographical. One warehouse roof

Lifts off in the 'throw-me-something' city,
City of flesh-pressed crowds, slow passing
floats. --It was always not about things:
the slow rush like first-time drunk, pretending

to belong: French Quarter bars, girlie-show
pasties and pubics, but nothing
like the wind that blew the garbage can relentless; the mind
Blotto! The whirling debris, the wind before

the rush to write, before the urge to be,
the spirit, body, mind, being, blown away.

Alfalfa

The Irish Channel, New Orleans

Walking-dead's a prisoner
about to die. That's his case,
Alfalfa, Camp Street barfly
The morning zombie, pale as flounder.

His homeless stink's beyond compare. I smell him
near the gate. Grandmother doesn't care
She makes him eat, sits him on the stairwell
listens to him suck his food, gives him carfare.

Where's he going? Only his radar knows--
Some alley way or park's deserted bench.
I am the last recalls he comes and goes
His staggered search, the thirst he couldn't quench,

And hear Alfalfa's heart stop quicker than
he hit the pavement, as if I'm there
the absent observer, a newsman
Noting undying thirst for life elsewhere.

Off to no ends

Off to no ends. Never lost
except at home. My great
grandmother sits all day
rocking outside
the one room she lives in, her mind
a package when the gift is gone.
Empty time
sits with her on the porch, eats her age away.

One midnight I knew
it wasn't wrong to wake my grandmother that her mother's dead.
What woke me?
ESP? Transcendent meaning?

I saw
The lights go on, doors open, deepest sleep.

Noninferential

I have found no way to will it,
transcendence I was told helps, and I have worked hard
to prove the point; glimpsing an instant the true knowledge of nothing
certain but sure, when I shivered the way through alleys and swamps with inner sight
for guide, until pressure to count time and tell tales imposed
bravura erected in the climbing heights of small meanings
where vague extravagance emerged outlandish
under the claim of 'best' days, nights, I lost
touch with the unseen, the projected
known without knowing, without
how- to-let-it-happen; these days
aware of those visions that I
learned not to trust now
I see them threatened
in ways I only
at this point
infer.

Gossip and black robes

A child familiar with gossip and black
Robes a priest at the corner hunchback
 Who knew the nuns who broke St. Bridget's rule.

Fire's catastrophe on my way to school
I spied the stretchers with their bellies
watermelon round habits in the alleys.

Ambulances wheeling past; sirens scream.
Islands of indulgence, impious dream:
Their lonely moments when desire burgeons.

The holy plunge into the font that opens.
The origins of the world painters paint,
Woman's darkest reaches, night's deviant saints.

Triolet

Men call it mystery the origin's opening:
Courbet conceives the face as covered

All else nude. For Rodin Iris goes flying
Headless, the messenger spread-eagle, daring

to show all, the thing itself, gaping,
hairless, no deception; nothing covered.

Known, yet unknown: desire's opening.
Men call it mystery even uncovered.

Two kids beneath their parents' robes

Mr. Ragusa next door throws dishes.
Mrs. Ragusa climbs the wall.
He lacks the grit to pass his barroom friends.
I count the flights of china flying Friday nights.

Regular nights they laugh out loud as if
Two kids beneath their parents' robes,
And after Friday fights pick up the porcelain,
Forgive unkind curses. --How life starts

to stop and starts up again! Each morning
listening to their love song readymade,
Not taking sides, feet on either bias of the seesaw,
One learns how both depend on something else.

Ice boiling

Ice
In boiling water, she is
He tells her

Erotic
Stories – the Perfumed Garden, cult of Q, story of
O. His hand

In her candy
Opening
Ajar.

Heirs to Catullus

Crawling up the stairs she bangs the broom
handle on my door, then throws a dime
at me to call the Liquor Store for wine.
Raucous renters underneath my room.

They died after I moved. I still hear them,
Poisoned by each other's pain unbearable,
One another's each other inseparable,
Their nightly screech-words coughing phlegm.

Sometimes -- noon-time – descending rickety stairs,
They emerge: Love's lovers, arms entwined,
The rage that broke their dishes re-defined.

Heirs to Catullus: love's *Odi-et-amo* hatred
At the door, happily lost in an endless war.

Hawking news to hurried cars

Hawking news to hurried cars, I am runt
to White Castle's crowd. The swivel barstool
hits eye-level. On the counter I hunt
Indian head pennies, my newspaper pool

garnered between cars, the red-light whip-through,
tough-looking crew-cut kid, dangling cigarette,
the scene like it's a shadow, yours but not you,
nor *déjà vu*, not then nor quite yet here yet

somewhere beyond an inkling, recall's trick;
 bogus bard of the caffeine crowd, blatant
street kid, resting from running: the quick
sales, the accretion of drivers, instant

faces, not even counted except in change
In out, open closing, the fast exchange.

Thanksgiving

I lived for the New Orleans YMCA. Boys swam
Naked then sneaked peeks through clouded windows
at visiting girls in the showers undressing. But
what a treat--when we learned one Thanksgiving turkey

would be the prize to the best young swimmer
swimming two miles a day for ten days! The first days
my friend, John Youmans, we paced each other
neck and neck. Nine days I endured knowing I was

Losing, gradually—a body length then two, finally
the whole pool. I hadn't a chance for the prize
I meant to gift my grandmother: that coveted
bird. On the last day, I waited for him, doubting

Till the last minute why he wasn't there. No use
Thinking about it knowing the prize for me was lost
though grandmother wouldn't miss it; she didn't
Know my secret. John didn't show.

I coasted the final two miles easily sprinting the last
Thinking he told his mother; she must have said,
"They need it more," and argued the prize
Meant to win the glow in grandmother's eyes.

We never talked about it. He mumbled something next
Day, as I stole my way into the movie house without
Him (he was too straight to cheat). I missed him there
Beside me in the dark, still glad not to pay the price.

Lifeguard on duty

Under twice,
he drifts toward foggy bottom.

I heave half of him over, then
up the slippery tiles the other half.

"I was OK! Why did you help me?" "I was OK!" he spit out flat
on his face after I'd pulled back
his engorged tongue, pumped his lungs, sweated 15 minutes.

Should I have let him sink into the slow waters, drifting off
A swollen log down to the cave of the last lepidoptera?!
Like a turtle, I might have approached more cautiously, taken my time.

So here's the coda of this stanza set:

Reptiles in the brain brawl; life's adverse--
Goodwill and hate seesaw, and verse
is polymorphously perverse, with or without rhyme,
leaps from ethical acts into dubious crime.

Buried in the mind's backyard

The "Cactus Flower" movie dug it up.
I watched young Goldie Hawn as 'Toni' get worked up
As some become when hopes disintegrate,
Close the windows, multi-lock the door

Turn on the gas lie down; determined to destroy
distress. But then (it hit me then) saved by a boy
(a striking young man, of course, in an emerging plot)
who smelled the truth outside her room

and broke a window, crawled in; saves her life.
The young man had a script. I didn't—just a kid, six
Or so, I pounded on the kitchen door. As I had known
When my great grandmother died, I knew again

Some dreadful wrong, that stark reason why
my mother locked herself inside, her quiet cry
above the faintest hiss and peculiar smell
companies give to gas. I yelled and yelled

and kicked the door until she let me in
sobbing as I turned knobs off, let the air in.
Later beat my head against the wall; "lights
Out" meant go-to-sleep man of the house.

Disillusionment of the movie usher

His grammar school puppy-love, she hands him
Her ticket to go in, not knowing who
She doesn't see, the boy her life outgrew
He stands there, motionless, once heart's whim,
A movie usher now, uniform frayed trim.
Her girlfriend reels off their later dates' rudiments,
Girl chat. He almost says her name, "Aren't you…?"
But then the ticket's torn; the houselights dim.

Break time, his relief sneers, "Easy screws".
Ouch! What happened to his fixed ideal?
He visualizes, grits his teeth, her flawless
Wet kisses in a dark spot going down
On and on he repeats the scene, scarcely hears
The background Looney Tunes. That's that!
Doesn't even checkout where she sat.

My Grandmother at the Library

Her life's untempered still.
In summer she'll drop reserve and coolly telephone
Enemies she's made to make it up.
"Did you know Aristippus
thought motion happiness?" She'll slump and laugh,

Her husband sang. When 'Faustus' left for Baltimore,
He promised, "I'll be back," and was—
For scores. Forty
years or more she's kept Madame Butterfly locked up.
Remembering,
she mumbles, *I'd rather be then what I seemed*
or out of this and dreams.

The labeled speechless mouths she talks to
understand death's a stoppage
sticks dust in jaws. "The world's no stage
but starts and quits!" she raged that day her son-
in-law tried to pledge her soul to Christian wits.
"Dirt's dirt," and that's what I'll be when you
pray for me!"

Last closing time at the library her daughter
caught her hunched on Revelations. Aside,
the desk attendant clicked his lips, "She won't move
that knee if it's not fixed."

Today she drags a Frankenstein hip as she unshelves
Isadora Duncan's acts, then carried off the show
She clapped inside. "Energy
Is Delight," she nods, and doubles
Over—on and off into the dancer's dance.

Spyglass hotel

Acapulco, 1959

The spyglass hotel:
hammocks and cots, thatched and open air. The waves

Right there: Acapulco's beauty then
No more:

'El Catalejo' -- one dollar nights, the see-to-the-bottom swimming
Clean. Lustrous in our 20s, years

Before nature's retreat, before it seemed ever to be defeated,
Before the abstracted wireless talkers in the air.

The waves wash up easy ocean
Riders, gambling in *the wabe*.

It couldn't last. But for that while
We fanfared in the sand.

Trash now; the human
Capital's beach. The hotels rise.

Bygones die. I pull the curtain but cannot
block the view.

Bones and Lavish

Und lassen dich, zu keinem ganz gehörent.

Five nights before we quit you caterwauled
"Take me!" then sank your hips and beat the air
for air. The echo swells in me sting-quick
and stays: love's after-flashes: chronic pain.
I pleaded your desertion. You abstained.
The bar judged us divided We shook free
and courted single beds to double us in sleep.
I live on bones and lavish. Life is cheap,

Life is cheap in D.F. "Give me beans," a dark-
shawled woman squalls. The Thin Coyote market brims.
Dogs and boys skirt baskets full of color; smells
compete. My Spanish wife's neat waist flows like her
voice. Up and down the aisles we buy to hoard
our Rubaiyat at home. Bread, wine and cheese
bring us together every other meal.
In Mexico all the world takes whatever it can steal.

I spot a double image, real as life:
Picasso paints one woman in her moods;
Nerval writes one mood's many women.
I split the picture: ends, old bits of both
kaleidoscope. This is my day. I dance, shifting
styles and fix my sights on now a thousand legs
in Paris. Lil, the Naturalist at Reims, relays
her like by looks. That lasts seven days.

The first time I saw Ann, she shrugged, "What am I
for, if not a man?" in love with Donne. That
Spring I woke covered with a girl named June,

or Gel. Jimenez said it: I can't remember.
New York later, Leda. But these fall fragments.
Divorce's lash strips memory: birth after
birth of jointed shocks. Still in Mexico
my new wife's hair reflects the sunlight's rainbow.

Home-leave

Back on home-leave my last visit, had I known.
Her smallness surprised me, her tough delicacy.
My grandmother and I scratched out my teenage years
Like cats trespassing territories.

But that last day in New Orleans, shopping
I bought a ten-pack box of Nestle bars for two
French chocolate-addict friends. Back
in her double-camelback exhausted house

Where had she put them? I had a plane to catch.
My anger cursed her in particular "damn you!"
"But who could want so much?" was her defense; she'd
Put them back, regretful she had caused me pain.

Such pettiness! Now it's no use. She cannot hear
this expiation's effort. So why put down myself?
Words that mimic D.H. Lawrence and the "Snake"
He threw a stone at. The years slide by. This hurt,

I have written of it some dozen times,
asking, Better to curse at all the world
Than miss one last show of love? Under this thin
veneer of understanding hard wood.

Spring wings punctuate the backyard sky.
The brain cells fix that petty aim to satisfy past friends,
now also out of reach. Twisted in this wingless dirge
I watch what's in the grass, the contracting earth.

Icy stairs

Icy stairs...
there it is, pain, not yet
known fully, too

unexpected. How it strikes
the instant body meets concrete, as when
an aimless child swings

fingers in your eye! How swift, there it is
underneath the edgy laugh, the hidden hurt
hanging effervescent, that dark spot

below the water's wave or
at the bottom where we fight for air. As if
a jouster's lance hit home

deeper than a hornet's sting.
Or splinter in foot's arch, the stepped-on
Catfish spine. Or barefoot, hidden in

the grass the bee defending turf exchanging hurt
for hurt. Slivers of broken glass cut into nerve, days weeks
mending, the frozen fall.

Unfinished sestina

We rode the St. Charles streetcar. That's not gone
But the camelback house and her both dust.--
The city razed the house for Algiers Bridge,
A double-camelback whose preservation's past.--
She'd keep me up at night, talked of principles:
"Stand straight; help the poor; walk like an Indian."

Her dicta track me now like an Indian.
Poor woman suffered delusions, husband gone,
Ranted at walls, but held to principles,
Which youth today wipe off like bookish dust:
Flotsam, jetsam, values of the past;
Next generations blare across their hip-hop bridge.

Her commands posed challenges to bridge:
Her heritage lost, history's warrior Indian;
She extolled our uncles in gold-leaf frame, past
Heroes, old accolades, events long gone.
A former world laid waste -- ashes and dust.
Not much left, except her fix on principles.

She argued what they meant, her principles:
To honor women, help the old, to bridge
The color gap. Once seated in the streetcar's dust,
"You see that lady standing?!" her 'Indian'
Jumped up (Southern manners not yet gone.).
The lady sat. The conductor walked past,

"Lady, see that sign behind you?!" What's past
Remains: Grandmother's love of principles,
She moved the "No colored" sign, composure gone,
And snapped "Now move me, young man?!" That's the bridge

Her grandson watched, quieter than an Indian.
I hold that memory like pure gold dust.

She wasn't much at cleaning household dust.
Her life embodied the future not the past,
Fought for the rights of blacks, the Indian.
Fearless acts revealed her strong-held principles,
Courage that stood against the caustic bridge.
The world's still split, the person gone.

New Orleans and the Neighborhood

It was a time of nicknames, streetcars, desire,
tree climbing, running loose, jousting giants, snow
balls in summer, sweat, slapping female
mosquito blood spots, spiders under the house

perched on brick stilts to deal with floods, rivers
of cats and dogs, one fierce hare hissing mad
on the upstairs balcony, pigeons in two
back rooms newspapers full of pigeon shit

the raccoon in a makeshift cage, one duck
one dog ate up, a mouse aflame no hope
burning in the cardboard box the next door
kids squealed to see it trapped quick cooked

the dog they caught and cut its tail too short.
I hear the neighborhood's gone down since then.

Motherboard

My first father-in-law's first wife died
It was unbearable, he said. He saw her eaten
up in flames, too late, too late. Who knows

such pain, and why? Then gradually facts fade.
I sit tight with my hands cupping
the motherboard; watch my wife watch woods

cluttered with recall. I invent her story,
how she swims through simulated waves; tides
repeat and crash before her eyes. Her life mostly

lived. Others step into her thoughts. I see
her passion on the edge of fire. Her hopes
cocooned in adjusted warmth.

New Orleans April

Alice Moser Claudel, Poet, Editor, Mother (1914-1982)

It's summer-hot this New Orleans April.
Laid out in an open, quiet gazebo
Her poetry friends prepared this last goodwill:
Over the rainbow Alice in wonderland.

I watched her when she wrote those early years.
Divorced, she languished for a lover's charms,
My father gone a gambler in arrears.
She feared her mother's fate, her thighs' alarms,

Dreading age's weight spelled hope's defeat.--
What's a man who was once a boy to feel,
Isolated incidents—small tears, conceit,
Who knew her vaguely, living life surreal

House devil street angel, training to compete.--
Still thin, she escaped the Irish Channel,
Our corner named for muse Calliope.
She left; I hardly noticed; life went null.

Now her mass's here, gigantic -- one final haul
To grates in Metairie's marble sites. Death-winds blow
A stench that hits me, grabs my throat, remains
That part the stagnant from the flow.

Deeper than the grave

Alice Moser (Claudel), (1914-1982)

I.

I should have dug deeper than the grave.
You disappeared but were never gone.
How could I know you left to me "the cave

where your storms can still blow free
from anonymous silence of the grave?"
Where hope of immortality bred poetry.

II.

Off with your new two-sided man ticked
by my childish whistling: jealous, strict,
hateful at home, socially a fool but

who stood against the KKK--unsung.
I've come to closure, those breakneck
past impressions, blanks, but where

erasures left their mark, imprinted
with your praise of beauty, depth in poetry,
awed at the core, life at six and sixty more.

III.

Your Vieux Carré literati afternoons--
amusing myself in Brocato's ice cream parlor
your son a dog under the tables chasing itself solo.

Even now I dream dreams of dreams, not
half awake to what some claim as "real,"
where 'get and spend' take charge

where education's arm leads to the end
identified by what one does, not many-armed
beyond the possible, beyond always.

> IV.

Growing apart I hardly noticed us
increasing in size each summer's visit;
I still goosing girls in streetcars winning

swimming meets, medals on the mantle
lifted off by bums who settled in
once your mother dropped dead on her front

room floor. My life undefined except
what hopes early marriage promised: to be whole
as when I learned to play with words.

> V.

Who cares what meaning's true, ideas
caught in a phrase or two with life at stake,
the absolute image in fabricated digits

to please the self and the subject matter.
You were always there, a letter or two
a year, enclosed five dollar bills, signed "Love."

In time a bureaucrat abroad I sought
to play the game to win
inroads into poverty. Years and years

of that, and then more words to educate
myself about the enriching rich, ignorant
as I was a beginner untutored in rubbing

sticks for fire. And now the ever
climbing shadow grows, the anonymous
silence, "the low pale light".

VI.

Humanity may disappear the curse
of greed, the spills of oil and threats
to kill ourselves in one gigantic hecatomb

that bio-gift and virus of technology's desire.
Who cares what's true, the meaning's clear
fate's in power's hands; gods flee

that never were, except in hearts
that set care free, but now the heart shrivels,
conflict beyond the possible, beyond always.

I never fought with you outright but held
Inside, the hateful love you left me
here as ever in this darkening, this

image mixed in metaphor. The Sun
descends, disappears never
completely so deeply as the grave.

Where did it go?

For Seymour Gresser, Sculptor

Where did it go? Like Villon's vanished snow
How fast; what's there to know? Desires to be,
To love? What's left is art: wood, paper, trash.

Faces in the crowding mass hurtling
On, we see each other pass. What didn't last
Remains. Wishes tighten their Venus grip,

The nymphs we didn't grasp, their heart-shaped hips.
Volcanic lava rolls across our path.
The love of flesh, that's much of where time went!

The rest is chips in stone, unwilling words
Thoughts, pictures left behind. Lunch on the lawn:
A naked woman with black bow-tie beckons.

Maddened by Sirens, even now.
Hear them sing! Hear them howl in the mind!

Our lady of prompt succor

At unease with each other, on his turf
in Chalmette, my step-father and I
review the fields where Jackson's sundry
low-life rogues, sharpshooters, pirates, shot

(sitting ducks) the redcoat British. Nearby,
a churchyard packed with tilted graves weathers
time. "Our Lady of Prompt Succor" looks on
unmoved. Above, the landed Moon highlights

The shaded stone slabs. No matter where they died,
battlefield or home, the names are hard to read.

Winter firewood

The butter on my breakfast dish flies off,
A clumsy man but quick I catch it,
fingers yellow spread before it hits the floor
(Tai Chi years pass by in one slow breath).

But not so quick, I also knocked the angel
Magnet off the fridge, the one almost forgot:
Arny's, a Men's Store, a piece of cloth ripped from
The coat I bought when he was there, a friend

Life cancered out before his time. Gives me
The shivers. The cold in Guanajuato
Where I thought he'd die; or Paris where women
Lodged love daggers in his heart. So many hellos

Goodbyes. New York, before the end
He sold firewood in winter as cancer
Burned him up. I missed his last goodbye.
He wrote me only that the clinic's clean.

One after another friends fall by, a few
Remain, one's 82 or more by now....
I smear the butter from my hand on bread,
Appetite aimless probing; all's been said.

Mortality

To my sculptor friend, Seymour Gresser

The blood coughed in your handkerchief
Is not on my sleeve; I wipe away the thought.

'You see I'm dying?!' You say.
I see your body knows

What the mind cannot forget: mortality.
In the wood you carve broad Indio faces

Mexican faces you shape each
One embraces life

Indelibly slow; images unfold, faces
Weathering weather, blind gods exposed.

Fighting in the streets, Paris '68

Between the CRS 'Darth Vedas'
In black, batons at the ready, the urge to kill

The students, their fired-up sympathizers erase
the slogan singers: "Le pouvoir est dans la rue!"

Forgotten? not entirely. My second wife and I
nothing then two lives backed against the Sorbonne

Wall, all entries tight; panicking we watched
the truncheons cut through the parting mass.

The Law School relenting opened one door, one minute
Time enough to crowd squeezing bodies through,

climb the stairs, fall prostrate on the floor, acrid
World War I teargas pouring in. Screams

Below the broken windows: Goya's 'No hay remedio!'
Knew worse scenes in Spain long years before.

At dawn; Darth Vedas gone. -- Off the floor
through tight-lipped streets, we hurry staring

ahead and back, toward children fast asleep. Fighting
in the streets again; why had we come this far?

I double-ear the pages in our books and thoughtless
tear out jokes, recipes and ads from magazines,

leave her nights to find the day's relief, playing
in a fiction underlined with rapid writing on the wall.

*The CRS, Compagnies Républicaines de Sécurité, are the riot control forces and general reserve of the French National Police.

The honey hardened

The honey hardened.
The usual story.
The fairy queen
Spread forth children.

I had no idea
what marriage meant: the every day
of it. I am witness to its wound:
the slow breaking of an ankle

that's the sound who hardly hears it
for the noise inside.

Weekends

Danny Kaye in the Catskills
flings his ballerina into the air.
Near-sighted, he cannot see her as she goes up.
Soon she, far-sighted cannot see him as she unravels down.
Crash bang! There you have it.

We live together weekends
Seldom in sync.

Middle of nowhere

Arrive's a magazine the Amtrak trains
Leave for the bored, time-passing passengers
Like me, but not like me, stopped inbetween
Somewhere and Newark I simply doze, I

Seldom remember dreams but there I was
Gripping tight each bounce, in a jeep, the jungle,
admiring jaguars, 4-wheeling in the red
dust outside Nayarit, and then, who was it

running zigzag fleeing war's bombardment,
Living in caves, drowning in the Yellow
River look, a million, billion dug graves
For me, for I was many more than thought.

A hesitant start, the train shakes awake,
Arrive's a last resort: a look at the world's flat maps,
The train starts and stops and I am forever
in the middle of nowhere approaching Newark.

One wave goodbye

At the bottom of the poverty pyramid
My uncle Julio found his fortune,
bought low sold high to those unable

To pay full price. But then grew bored, let go
The reins... with profits close to zero
His wife took over. But business tied her in knots.

She sought release in forbidden spots,
Finally riding off one afternoon
With a Harley growl and one wave goodbye.

She left her dull cocoon
Roared toward the superhighway
Left Uncle Julio half-awake in pajamas standing

in the driveway cursing love, pissed he'd let his life go slack
Caught napping, didn't wave back.

On the train and off what's left is time

Headed north the backgrounds blend,
Passengers sleep--some keep a steady stare.
It's all straightforward, yet suspended.
Pending New York; all else's nowhere.

Who endures the scene, gets ready for the dash.
I grip my bags, check the dark dried
Apricots she fancies, dump my cumulated trash,
Go forward, roll and bump. I stake which side

To exit. Next, the rush (dammit, escalator out!).
The Station overflows, the zigzag starts,
bit by bit advance, fumble for my subway card.
Then, almost home: flights of stairs and... sweetheart's

Not there! Kaput to uplift! Hyper drop!
No kisses no expected hug. It's late;
She's gone to Pioneer I guess to shop.
Exuberance and excess left to wait.

I unwrap; unpack the mundane. Bummer!
My special gifts look small, one's dented.
I change from shoes to slippers, lose fervor.
It's all straight forward still suspended.

Persimmons

Persimmons drop late fall,
I gather them up, sweet pink.
This small

Forest called woods as I look up
The sky bares down: one
Round expanse horizons limit.

Wildlife is less, less than wild:
Birds, squirrels, the occasional turtle,
The occasional deer, buck, doe,

Dogs on leash, the morning's human predators
Hold back the reptiles in their brains.
The leaves mainly oak, a tulip tree

Or two, a hickory here and there, a birch,
An elm, a noisy walk the leaves make,
Shush and crackle, until I come round about

Where I started with
Persimmons, their tree thin bodied
In Maryland, not like in New Orleans

Where trunks lend big adventure to the boy
Who hides inside their crotches not
Seen above the passersby, who knows

Not to pick them green, best when shaken
Loose or fall, best not stepped on sweetest
When the tree goes bare.

Icarus again

For Andy

The many ways to go in life or out of it:
turns in the road, taken not taken,
bumps against a shoulder, wall,
or gun, gas, dramatics while they last,

Hitler's holocaust or *habeas corpus* writ
too late. Or then again like Icarus who flies
into the blaze, this time not pilot error:
engine failure. Others live on, write

how he disappeared in desert sand--
a streak across the sky let's say, because
I didn't see him go. All I know is rumor, the buzz
around the quad: he went airborne and died, one

thought most blessed, even I who cared less
what's coming or why. Or what it meant to care.

II. RED WINTER

Red winter

Frozen wires hang in perfect arc.
The precise Sun
steeped in snow
wipes out the flawed. Perfection

is. Or is it?
Underneath's the blemish
writing hides. The cursor

like Procrustes cuts distended gaze. In the room a woman
stretches, reconstructs itinerant truth with an itch.
I wrestle with red winter, routing

Imperfect thoughts inside white frames. None
Escapes what's cold as ice. Words
control the way snow falls perfectly.

Daisies

"She loves me; she loves me not;" petals
Picked by bands of love-sick Sidneys; and
Catullus long before. Who doesn't know
The song!? I'd sooner be the subject

Alba ladies elevate with bawdy hands
hurried as dawn-songs hail the nightingale,
when Sun's up scrambling out--a kiss quick
promises pending next rendezvous.

Is love love for love's sake--not a pretty face?
Or is it at first sight Anne's yellow hair?
The noble give it up for honor, some
wreck it outright, Wilde's sword, or betrayal.

Long life's resigned, opines Phil Larkin's poem
Leaving luck of ache and promise
To "others undiminished somewhere" inbetween
The pleasure never ending and the pain.

I wouldn't kick old poets when down and out…
Let them be resigned to "others," they don't know
While I keep tabs on cute behinds, and marking 'yes
or no' count daisy petals just for show.

Everything I told her

Everything I told her that late evening
As the skies made stars in the bright
Dark on the outskirts of Accra, was a lie
Pointing up how Orion arrives at night

tossed into the heavens by gods who wept to see him
pierced by Apollo's arrow, a shot that burned
with jealous rage as Orion swam careless...
And the girl's name I forgot who spurned

Apollo's advances. --You must be a great man,
She said. I breathed in that moment forming
The world out of imagination, the way myth
Must have emerged as when sky-gazers charmed

Their brides gesturing with words, talking them
To bed. Even her name Naomi bloomed
Open into 'Dahomey'. She embraced my make-believe
Happily matched in the dark, consumed

As the sky sparkled, and the warm night held
adventures to be told; the world became ours
As stars turned into nothing's left, all else
On the outskirts--notes on sketchy memoirs.

It was splendor nonetheless, those times
That count for much and little now, just rhymes
Assemblages of seduction written in old age
Lies and other premeditated crimes.

Outstanding in Penn Station

Penn Station
faces like dogs

chasing trails, hurried
kisses

goodbye, on the way
mobile phoning. One woman

looking around stops me from scanning, who
doesn't

wave, no rush
to hugs.

She hesitates
outstanding

in a pretty
Sunday of likelihoods.

In line at the grocery

Enamored of the produce colors
In line at the grocery,
Carrots in my face, vegetables like urges
Tightly wrapped, I stand in place,

Patient, distant, stuck
In daydreams, attached to chance, I shift
To places we used
to meet: parks, offices, afterwords. Lost

In projected scenes, I hold you in my mind,
Erotic, unreal, multiple images, thoughts
Better than none, I think. Better to
Have been, still to be, next in line.

She walks into the room

Das Ewig-Weibliche Zieht uns hinan.

She walks into the room stark naked.
I embrace her. Then she's gone...

Bangalore, Accra, Lahore

names I read out loud. On the floor
spread maps, fluctuate and soar, open

doors. She

walks into the room
a figment, invisible, not to be ignored.

"The Carnal Prayer Mat"

Li Yu. "The Carnal Prayer Mat" "(Rou Putuan"1657),

Li Yu wrote to a friend his intention
to please, "make people laugh"--displayed Chinese
society in a state of undress--
"for the world's a vast erotic work of art."
His novel *Rou Putuan* (Mat of Flesh),
a moral tale he claims, entices,
informs, targets 'the heart of the flower,'
with delightful euphemisms parts sex
from the vulgar, 'observes the flowers
from horseback,' 'approaches the fragrant
bamboo,' 'plays the flute,' 'the jade whisk.'

The main character Vesperus 'plows the fields'
aided by the Knave his go-between
For whom a vulva came to resemble
A kitchen utensil. So goes the story
From erotic adventure to adventure
Until the end, when V.'s wife, in a brothel
Hangs herself. Reborn, V. undergoes
castration, seeks monastic life. The Knave too.

In sum, I wonder, does joy require
the seismic tumble? The whirlwind morning-
after? Face-to-face together ever. Or is bliss
one long solitude transcending flesh?-- to live for
Bodhisattva's benefit? Who knows?

One thing's sure. In 'the heart of the flower'
billions now release their butterflies
in search of fragrance,' unfettered by restraint
or common sense, while infinite floating seeds
that inundate the earth blot black the sun.

Marie-Denise Villiers: self-portrait

In the Metropolitan Museum (1774-1821)

Framed and intense she's painted herself, her left hand
Holds a sketch pad tilted up, the right ready. Dressed in flowing white,
soft but targeted as if inviting the onlooker to pose for her, as if
her palette captures whoever stands before her.

About her there's the slightest tease, one foot out
from under, the other hidden beneath her floor-length elegance.
So slight a smile, her small nose, blue eyes, her curls of hair
cascade. Stunning how the impression does not stop but flows.

In the Parisian window behind her two small figures in formal dress;
Are they in love or desiring love? Her smile reveals the onlooker's thoughts.
How many times that day I turned back, sought her out, and left,
Nothing fixed--apart from a postcard by my desk,

Traces of her shaded sky, her creviced dress, the hint of what's been
missed, the clue to what she means, her look beyond expertise.

Delmore Schwartz

Here's how I think of him, a favorite poet:
At the end of life a lone
wolf in Times-Square's wilderness, gutterized,
crawling under garnered rags. Bedbugs in his nights, no recourse

on 42nd street: "Escape!" the bottle cries.
In flight, his images bend light bulbs
frozen in art's ice. He liquefies life's chains,
the city's rush scrimmaging for gain.

In his veins Bohème sings the stars asleep
against the blur of noisy bars.
Only his companions remain: dog, bear,
dark alleys, dead ends, the sky's edge

where he stumbles off. The apple, fig, whatever
they offered him, the taste was hell.

"Lottery dream"

Inspired by a Fred Folsom drawing of the same title

She's rich. Rich! Transported

    In a gesture -- bone-bare, pipe-rollers
    In her hair, the captured
    Moment. No more poverty
    No more ....

        We see behind her
Fixed facts:
The basic room: a mirror hung by kitchen wire, a fire
Extinguisher on the wall, a rumpled bed, one sheet thrown
Back: raw mattress. What matters?

For her
This ecstasy, her frame of mind;
For us

              Observers we

Admire how the artist exposes
A truth, how
Dreams can stir our being
Into dreams, the dream what if

We wake up in the thought: yes, yes
"I'm a winner!" Walk off richer and content.

Angel bird

La Castañeda, Mexico's former national insane asylum; dismantled in 1968.

I volunteered to do some good for nothing,
Donated time to the Quakers' cause: to aid
Those lost in Castaneda's looney bin:
Eight Wards: bare bones, raw concrete, men,
Women, children, even epileptics
(Their heads in stitches dousing bloody floors!)

The Quaker team in disarray, no plan,
No place to start. They looked up for a sign.
I sent them home; assumed the mission
Mountains of boxed gifts for Christmas
Just past; walked into the Children's Ward, stood
Toward center, called for ten to help me out.

They gathered in a room apart; I picked
Recruits, then turned to close the door and start.
I couldn't. There she stood, against my strength.
I pushed again. No luck. She simply chirped.
I let her in. Why not eleven, not just ten!
Until the end she stayed. -- I handed out Christmas cards

Flip-flops -- in January-cold La Castañeda --
Whispered to the crazed, moved from one to one.
Sadist wardens crowded them in tight line-ups:
They strike one badly, a nervous woman waving,
Blood already on this charity purpose;
I warned away the clubbers. – Then in the Men's Ward
the ten kids gone, except for my tweety girl,
I face two half-wit criminals, their smiles
Gold-toothed intentional. What now?! Tweety

Steps in front of me. Expecting blood, more
Blood, I watch as her hisses halt them. Ferocious
Hawk, she backs them off, this angel bird.

What could have been was not. She saved the day,
My synecdochic ass. Was it grace or luck?
I let her in. Why not eleven not just ten.

What's more difficult?

In memory of Gil Cuatrecasas, painter

Over his shoulder as he sketched
stems for his Catalan-born
father, expert scientist, lover of plants,
who knew his own bright precise abstractions
would later drown in the Contemporary Arts
Museum basement flooded by summer rains?

Crises happen: the Corning Museum
Hurricane Agnes, upstate New York 1972
the Arno River rise in Florence 1966.
A summer storm, rising tides, life works gone.

A young master greedy of his work,
reluctant to sell even to the few who knew
his skill, his art, his vision beyond the commonality
of names, the flitting back and forth, learning
from dried up leaves and petals. When
his father said "Look again, now look again," he looked
seeing slowly until epiphany, sight's
thinnest whispers in the world,
nodes and internodes, true style, sexy
stamens, ovaries and all that could be seen.

"Desks bobbled like harbor buoys,"
his paintings like rafts that couldn't save the day.
What good's insurance even if they had had it.

Yeats wrote about a friend
whose art came to nothing, "that is
most difficult." "Nothing" meaning

shortfalls to inspired intentions. But what when
brilliance is simply washed away! What's more difficult,
the critic's judgment or the rains
that flood museum basements?

From there he moved easily
to isolation, books lessening
the daily subdued hunger that once
nothing assuaged, he became a ghost
in Barcelona's roar, as if from under earth,
his mind made up its mind
to live outside art's urgent accidents.

Broken mirror

And did we know each other? I recall
A smaller person, strong, curvaceous; tall
Stories I told myself over the years,
A voice inside a body nobody hears.

"Truth" is no longer truth and "beauty" much
The same. Image isn't matter to the touch.
Together, talk tells what we haven't done:
Not kept in love nor married into "one".

That haloed face in fur-coat collar
Filmed in a broken-mirror; time's colder
Now. You talk of politics and read papers
In bed, stone silence about past capers.

Neither cared then what we knew or didn't know,
You were the id, I a different ego.

Graffiti

Blek le Rat, Banksy, and the Guerilla Street Artists

Michelangelo's David totes an AK47. Art
as action, a Baader-Meinhof complex
Of the mind: up against the wall with aerosol.
Runners in the mall, escapees from class. Art is war.
Fleeing the whistle, they paint on others' property.

"Sky's blue; life's beautiful," they quip. Rats (stenciled) run
Palpable and mute. Sheep stand pat, sleep-eyed.
Beggars lie wordless in their flight. Scene-faces stare:
Who at? --Goldman Sachs, Monsanto, United Fruit?
Those who bring the best to bear and terror too?

A sign of the new global, their art in life is life.
Its meaning meaning impermanent egos:
Freudian tits suckled by surreal daddies; it means
the world is mean. It means: rat silhouettes, ugly
undergrounds, blue-velvet wildlife, and sheep.

Guerillas without guns, their splash-state art's whatever
Shocks; the city's trash. Stenciled patterns repeat the theme:
Rats abound, and sheep. Asleep in the museums
Lifeless form hangs. Up against the walls outside aerosol
Drips as the moon climbs, as the sun drives home.

Dregs seldom seen haunt the eye. What's next? The TV
Box on metronymic man. Standing on prohibitions, feelings
that can't wait, guerilla life attacks. Sky's blue. Rats
Exit through gift shops, helter-skelter, terrifying,
We get the drift (just looking), life's a shiver.

Western Wind, the corollary

Anon, did you write "Western Wind"
in the trenches..., or was it
later at leisure affirming how it was--
your love in bed? Perhaps

you scraped it on a wall, a need you had
to scratch out chronic pain; or again perhaps
to calculate the cold, the fighting drenched.
What else did you write, Anon.?

What about the war itself, the other men?
What happened then? Did all your endings end
In ache? Did you ever make it back? Perhaps
You danced with death face down. Or do you still

roam the homeless streets, out of luck, your mind
sparkling in the small rain's muck.

Patuxent River flow

For Ralph Greenhouse, cellist and anthropologist

We sat, my friend and I, facing the wind
On an evening's bench, recalling the wrench
Of women past, the flaws, imposed failures,
How we die a little -- each passing breeze

Still lifts the spirit. See how we can squeeze
Out pleasure just from watching Patuxent
River flow into the Chesapeake. This far's
the measure of how far we've come -- to this

Bliss of being where we are enjoying
The bench the breeze, our embedded scars.

Storm's edge

I kicked a tree and wondered when it fell
To me to walk this way and not another
Day goes by but what things change.

What had I done? What's there to know
that knowing makes no difference? I walk the slow
Plank of wreckage, wavering, another

wingless dirge. Did heart opening under the covers
Close? I stand at the storm's edge, fear and the flesh
expand/contract. She is stark

reality it seems and I am where some nurtured spite
resides. I cannot see the forest but the hard
hurt, kicking at what will not change:

the sporadic chasm, the spiral flight,
the scalp's tight itch, the appetite's backbite.

In the house alone

Some die from fear their time will come.
I thought I'd buy a gun, and then?
Would I wear it in a holster? Just for fun?

An old man in a house alone a mile away ...
Drugged teens gone wild beat life

Out of him. Fear. Some call it paranoia: reality
Pushed to its extreme. In the house alone I listen.
A creaking, and the thought sneaks in.

Eros and Thanatos

I try to make them talk, these written words
but ask about their meaning, it's the same
(always): the boy's relentless lust and father death. All else's
pleasure parks of whispered intimacies, life's middle age.

Thus, these unwavering words, like music
rise and fall, redolent with odors of sex and death,
the Venus trap, the Phaedra itch, a child's
inherent hunger, the images of delectable thighs,
one's head between the pages—words
that tell how birds of prey let slip the prey.

Love's death is darkest for the young. And yet
life's funerals haul off those dangling in the air,
not yet devoured,
Prey to the screeching eagle and the heart.

Spring's already here!

What's there to hope for? Spring's already here!
My late profession deemed success, the tools
Life needs to function well in place. Each day
Sheer ecstasy to know plants breathe and me.

The microscopic flakes that winter piled
Up coated black with grime and melted down
Into the sewers, drinking water for another time.
Not all that washes out comes back again.

The season's ripe. No need for hope except
It's like my fall this year on icy steps
So swift, an instant! Then, not there! I guess I was
In air, so quick the concrete stair, no time

To hope I wasn't there, but there I was
That instant one split flash, grounded.
My hope's this final truth: I hope
It's not in spring, not too slow, and not yet.

Beyond belief

The Greeks, the Romans, Hindus, Turks, all
Call on gods for help because
deep shadows lurk beneath their faith. Many

Want to go on and on, in gardens high, on
sofa clouds, be part of something bigger, Almighty. God!
I know the urge. Nobody wants to die

Forever. It's too long, beyond belief.
I walk the streets, listen, look both ways, stop
At the edge where words expire, and wave

At honkers, praying as they go who curse
Against the daily rut, the solar system cataclysm,
the finite body, the pending unforeseen.

And in my disbelief I watch me gather stones
To place in threes along the window sill.

Conch shell

Where did it come from? The sea of course
I mean how did it come to me, the conch, this horn
Full of sounds resounding in the basement shell
Where I retreat, the underground, the under house?

I never feared my childhood but the salt
Thrown hot into the boil that festers still
I knew it then a dream world, much like this
With argument and particulars, dishes

In the sink insensate but still waiting
To be washed, the water paid for monthly,
The messages machined with urgency,
The reference books and sites, that same me

And not an 'other' me, but different shapes
That brought me here to hear the ocean break
Above the surface, loosened from beneath
Against its plates, rotation's pull and grind.

Despite the stillness Earth breathes out
Its motion, afloat in the changing spheres
The ever shifting fixities where human words
Pile up, repeated in one long exalting, painful

Din, the sound of conch shells calling one
Another, above the fray, underneath
The speechless poems, the trumpeting let loose
In blasts of burdens resounding and adrift.

In others' words

Not who he is but who he was
or will be what

who never knew him determine him to be
So he is

A future figment
a wisp of wind not strong enough

to lift the words
where he sits

invisible
on avenues squeezed with people hunched

to purposes like his
He shapes

his puzzle's piece
the scattered slow placement

of the landscape fabricating
how if at all he fits

in context like dark
matter's part of it, the picture

as a puzzle, the pieces in others'
words.

Notes

"Heirs to Catullus": "*Odi et amo*" *(I love and I hate)* is one of Catullus' best known statements to his love, Lesbia with whom he had a tempestuous affair. Lesbia is named in only thirteen of Catullus' *carmina*; however, she is implicit in 26, among which is the memorable elegiac couplet, carmen lxv, quoted herewith in full:

> "Odi et amo. quare id faciam, fortasse requiris?
> nescio, sed fieri sentio et excrucior."

"Patuxent River flow": The Patuxent River is a tributary of the Chesapeake Bay in the state of Maryland. There are three main river drainages for central Maryland: the Potomac River to the west passing through Washington D.C., the Patapsco River to the northeast passing through Baltimore, and the Patuxent River between the two.

"The Carnal Prayer Mat": Li Yu, author of *The Carnal Prayer Mat* "(Rou Putuan"1657), (Trans. By P. Hanan, NY: Balantine 1990).

"Eros and Thanatos": "Love and death" were believed by Sigmund Freud to be the two main central conflicting desires that drive human beings: the life drive involving urges toward survival, sex and propagation (Eros) and the death drive (Thanatos).

"Gossip and black": In the second-to-last line, "the origins of the world painters," reference is to Gustave Courbet's *L'origine du monde* (1866). See photo in *New York Review of Books*, Feb. 14, 2008, p. 31.

"Spyglass hotel" "El Catalejo" is Spanish for "The Spyglass." El Catalejo was the one and only "hotel" on Acapulco Beach in the mid-1950s. It was a thatched-roof habitat for young people mainly who were willing to sleep in the open air on cots or in hammocks.

"What's more difficult": Many works of art were destroyed by floods of 1976 in Galveston and Houston, Texas, and several artists, such as *Gil Cuatrecasas* lost their life's work (noted in *Texas Monthly*, August 1976).

"Angel bird": La Castañeda, Mexico's former national insane asylum dismantled in 1968.

"Buried in the mind's backyard": "Cactus Flower" = *Cactus Flower* is a 1969 comedic film directed by Gene Saks and starring Walter Matthau, Ingrid Bergman, and Goldie Hawn. The film is adapted from an earlier Broadway stage play, written by Abe Burrows, which in turn was based upon the French play *Fleur de cactus*.

"Weekends": Danny Kaye, born David Daniel Kaminsky to Ukrainian Jewish immigrants in Brooklyn named Jacob Kaminsky (father) and Clara Kaminsky (mother), Kaye became one of the world's best-known comedians (1913 – 1987).

"Paris 1968": The CRS refers to the 'Compagnies Républiques de Sécurité' which are the riot control forces and general reserve of the French National Police.